THE WOMEN OF MY LIFE

Barbara Wojtowicz

BookLeaf Publishing

India | USA | UK

Presentation by *BookLeaf Publishing*

Web: www.bookleafpub.com

E-mail: info@bookleafpub.com

ISBN: 978-93-5744-334-0

First edition 2022

For my future love.

ACKNOWLEDGEMENT

My profound thanks to my to oldest friends:

Olga - for your constant presence.

My Mum - I am only here because of You.
You made me out of clay, coal and sugar.

Thank you to Rachel for patiently checking
every single word and to Ania for
beautifully illustrating my words
www.aniapawlik.com @anek_dota

Rebirth

I was once

just meaningless dust.

A small stain of

blood and brain cells.

A vulnerable motion

of brightness and lightness.

Drifting

in the space of nothingness.

Bouncing from one astral body

to another.

Orbiting around black holes

and satellites,

with no intentions to dock,

or

settle down.

And one day between

the infinity and the Sun,

I found you,

MY EARTH.

Mother

You made me out of clay, coal and sugar.

Wrapped me in cotton and fairy dust.

Locked me in a glass snowball.

Protecting me against evil, rain and your

mistakes.

Now I am standing in front of you.

Made out of concrete, diamonds and salt.

I want to wrap you in cotton and fairy dust.

Lock you in a glass snowball.

Protect you against evil, rain and my mistakes.

Mo(A)(R)ning

I woke up on the wrong side of the bed.

Cold and light-headed.

My left sock and her husband were missing.

There was no coffee in the cupboard.

No water in the tap.

No signs of life.

I opened the window and looked down.

A bright yellow spot on the gray concrete.

His wife.

Her dog chasing after my pussy cat.

I smirked.

Some things will never change.

π

Like Biblical brothers-history likes to repeat

itself...

To life imprisonment in my own company

heavens sent me to.

Behind the bars of eternity I find my

reflection in the moon.

I see myself.

You.

Myself.

I try to make sense and cry out for answers.

I hope to see your smile on my lips.

You are the brown sparkle in my eye.

Childhood scar on my right knee.

Left hemisphere of my brain.

Freak of nature - Gods you may laugh!

Destiny - Gods beware!

Behind the bars of eternity I find my reflection

on the moon.

I see you.

Myself.

You.

Ruby

Blood still shimmers in the silver halo on your

head.

Once hot in your veins, full of life...

Now only clots...

Like withered moments full of regrets…

Sparkling like diamonds, rubies, and stained

glass.

Pockets filled with glitter and breadcrumbs.

Prayer and dance soothe you before dusk.

Your sore feet can no longer bear so many

sins.

Swirling in the white, soiled bed you wish us

happiness.

Cherry Blossom

Some people - you might think are eternal.

They stand proudly in the garden of life.

Indifferent to the gears of fate.

Time for them has stopped.

On the gray skin joy and hope is written.

Sorrow in between wrinkles covered with

powder carefully.

With a smile on your face you serve us

morning tea.

Cherry blossom outside the window begs us

to be young again.

G

My starting point

to which I keep coming back with joy.

To my Home...

To the bedroom with the stars on the ceiling.

To my favorite coffee in my favorite mug.

Sitting around the kitchen table.

Sunday lunch chewed with love and serenity.

Strolling the streets, we're going nowhere.

We can't say a word, yet we plan our future.

Heads in the clouds.

There is no thinking about tomorrow.

Life happens when we make plans.

∞

The feeling of losing your soulmate is like ten

million tiny paper cuts.

All over your body.

On a scale of 1 to 10; 1 being no pain at all

and 10 being the worst pain ever,

I would give it 8.

But on its side.

It cannot be measured.

It is infinite.

It is eternal.

A broken heart after losing your soulmate is like

a chronic disease.

There is no cure, but with time, you can learn to

manage your pain.

You can try to tame it like an animal but it will

always yearn for the wild.

Bad karma

What comes around goes back around.

All the bruises, all the pain.

You get back what you put out.

One day bad karma will get you.

'It will get you too', she said.

'It already did', I replied;

'When I met you...'

Soul sister

I remember the day you entered my life.

My eyes were still covered with glitter and I

couldn't see you properly, but I felt

your presence.

My soul welcomed yours, and you made

yourself at home.

The void in my heart was finally filled. I finally

had a sister.

Not blood related but spirit bound.

Blood isn't always thicker than water anyway.

In a field full of yellow suns, we stand together,

against all the elements.

We will not surrender!

We will never give up!

Childhood

Love smells like tomatoes in the green house,

roses, and freshly cut grass.

It smells like cake, baked every Saturday, Nivea

cream and roast chicken.

Love feels like starched sheets, icy cold wind

and warm, woolly slippers.

It feels like a scratch on my left knee, tummy

rubs and a summer breeze.

Love tastes like sunflower seeds, strawberries

dipped in sugar and peppermint tea.

It takes like bread and butter, cold tea and

homemade cough syrup.

Love sounds like whistling, birds singing and an
old train carrying coal.

It sounds like a pacemaker, the midday news and

Christmas carols.

Love is all the childhood memories locked away

in a wooden box.

In the purest form.

All the blissful moments, filled with laughter

and sunshine.

Unaware of what's to come.

Creation

They always warn you never to play with fire.

They tell stories about its catastrophic nature.

But they forget that each cycle of destruction

creates a cycle of birth…

So I set myself on fire.

I burnt all the bridges and I finally set myself

free.

Afterglow

The day you left me, for the first time I realised

That our fundamentals were never strong

enough to build a house.

The day you left me, for the thousandth time I

realised that

the potential of what we could have been was

only an illusion.

Just like the afterglow we used to dance to.

Holding on to the light that was already gone.

I was always too much and you were never

enough.

So you went to get less and I needed to find

more.

Bygone

From the top of the Atlas Mountains you look at

the world.

The valley where once you ran free is now

covered in concrete.

All the familiar faces and places are gone.

No one looks up and seeks the stars anymore.

Nothing around you feels like home.

The square where you sit still every night is full

of life...

Yet no one is truly living.

People are making noises but no one is really

listening.

Dried saffron in a glass bottle shimmers like
rubies.

Exotic fruit

She asked my name about four times a day.

When she asked for the fifth time, I lost my

patience.

Not with her but with God...

For allowing her beautiful mind to be turned into

mush.

She used to tell me a story of when she was

eighteen and thought a word

'lesbian' meant an 'exotic fruit'.

I told her that exotic fruits were my favourite,

but she would only smile and nod.

Coming out would make her even more

confused.

Every night she would ask about her mother, and

I would quickly change the

subject, pointing at random things in her

bedroom.

She loved that room.

The décor reminded her of her youth.

We would stare at her citrus print wallpaper until

she fell asleep.

Little angel

When I asked you about your favourite ice

cream flavour from when you were

little, you replied: 'fat free'.

You couldn't remember the brand but you

memorised the calorie content.

When I ate Jaffa cakes for breakfast you said

that I was #goals but secretly you

were hoping that you'd never be like me.

When I sat with you in the emergency room

after you swallowed five pills and

some batteries,

You said that your last meal would have been ice

cubes served on some cold,

winter air.

I thought you were joking but you said that

you were worried your body wasn't

going to fit in a coffin.

Pebble

I was so grateful when the infinite cosmos sent

you my way again.

I always knew, deep down that our story wasn't

quite finished.

There were still words unsaid, places unseen and

memories unmade...

but after all, the universe had a different plan for

us.

What I need you to know is that even though

you may not be my forever pebble, you were my

rock.

In a year where everything fell apart, we came

together.

I am glad that I once again walked this earth

with you.

Side by side.

Your footsteps left next to mine.

Maybe we will meet again, perhaps in another

life, in another realm.

I found shelter in your heart but I am still

looking for my home.

Not meant to be

We are not bad people but we are just not good

together.

We don't always elevate one another.

We don't always evolve at the same time.

Sometimes instead of growing old together, we

simply grow apart.

Magic beans

Fire, Air, Water and Earth.

My tribe, my people, my biggest fans.

We could not be any different.

Each one of us is unique, with a different set of

scars and experiences.

We dance together and we fight together...

or sometimes with each other.

They love me when I forget how to love myself.

They remind me that even though I might not

have the energy, I always have

the power to be who I want.

Conquer the world.

Ask for what I deserve.

And just like the magic beans on my window sill

I watch them grow every day.

Do not believe in storks

I never really believed in Santa, tooth fairy or

storks.

The story of the birds and the bees bored me to

death.

I would roll my eyes or pretend that I was

asleep.

My awareness didn't make me eager but it

definitely made me the coolest kid

on the playground.

Some may think that I lost my innocent years

but I disagree.

What I also didn't lose is my virginity at the age

of thirteen like most of my

friends...

I knew more about body autonomy than I knew

about body anatomy.

Male body anatomy to be precise.

I suppose I always knew not to waste my time

on unnecessary things.

First love

She had short hair, climbed trees and wore khaki

cargo pants.

The same ones my mum wouldn't let me wear as

'they were for boys only'.

My brain carefully connected all the dots and

gave me the green light.

She looked just like other boys so I guess that

made it all okay.

I didn't really question anything but how do you

even question something you

didn't know existed in the first place?

I couldn't find the right words to describe it all

so I just shrugged my shoulders

and called it love.

9 789357 443340